magic
ADD-A-STRIP
QUILTS

Barbara H. Cline

Transform Simple Shapes
into Dynamic Designs

C&T PUBLISHING

Text copyright © 2017 by Barbara H. Cline

Photography and artwork copyright © 2017 by C&T Publishing, Inc.

Publisher: Amy Marson

Creative Director: Gailen Runge

Editor: Lynn Koolish

Technical Editors: Susan Nelsen and Debbie Rodgers

Cover/Book Designer: April Mostek

Production Coordinator: Tim Manibusan

Production Editor: Alice Mace Nakanishi

Illustrator: Kirstie L. Pettersen

Photo Assistant: Mai Yong Vang

Instructional photography by Diane Pedersen of C&T Publishing, Inc.,
unless otherwise noted

Published by C&T Publishing, Inc., P.O. Box 1456, Lafayette, CA 94549

Library of Congress Cataloging-in-Publication Data

Names: Cline, Barbara H., author.

Title: Magic add-a-strip quilts : transform simple shapes into dynamic designs /
Barbara H. Cline.

Description: Lafayette, CA : C&T Publishing, Inc., 2017.

Identifiers: LCCN 2017009726 | ISBN 9781617455537 (soft cover)

Subjects: LCSH: Patchwork--Patterns. | Quilting--Patterns.

Classification: LCC TT835 .C5957 2017 | DDC 746.46--dc23

LC record available at https://lccn.loc.gov/2017009726

Printed in China

10 9 8 7 6 5 4 3 2 1

Acknowledgments

*To my husband, children, sisters, quilting
friends, and students, who continue to inspire
and challenge me in my quilting arena.*

*To my sisters, sister-in-law, daughters, and daughter-
in-law, who each made the project quilt variations.*

*To all the quilters in my classes, for sharing
their love and joy of quilting with me.*

*And to everyone at C&T Publishing—
Lynn Koolish, Susan Nelsen, Debbie Rodgers,
Alice Mace Nakanishi, and Tim Manibusan.*

*And thanks to RJR Fabrics and Northcott
for their beautiful fabrics.*

CONTENTS

PROJECTS

Slicing Squares

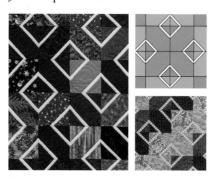

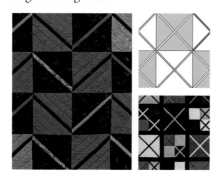

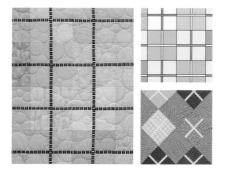

Slicing a Right-Angle Triangle

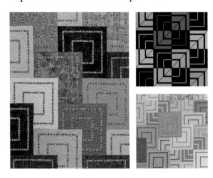

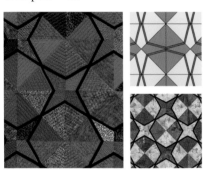

Slicing 60° Diamonds

Slicing an Odd Shape

The Family Sewing Retreat

Each year my mother, six sisters, a sister-in-law, and some of the nieces get together for a weeklong sewing retreat. Living many miles apart does not keep us from getting together each year for this event. Our family's sewing retreats have played a primary role in getting the next generation interested in sewing. We find a commonality in sewing and a community grows out of the interaction that occurs over the hum of sewing machines. These sewing retreats over the past eighteen years build family relationships as well. There can be anywhere from eleven to twenty-five people at a sewing retreat, it just depends on who can come and how many days they can attend.

I love the interaction between the four generations. My daughters and daughter-in-law know my sisters in a unique way that would have never happened if this gathering did not exist.

We bounce ideas back and forth as we sew. We have a large variety of talent to pull from: I may not know how to write but there is someone who can give me ideas for writing. The photographer in our group helps in photographing ideas for trimming and posting our pictures. The oil and watercolor painters help us fine-tune our color selections and help us understand why value is as important as color in quilt making. We all learn from each other and value each other. This not only happens in the quilting and sewing arena but it also happens in sharing our personal stories.

I love to take a quilt that I am ready to quilt to these gatherings and get four or five of the ladies around the quilt to each come up with an idea of how they would quilt it. From the input of each quilter there are so many different ideas. Then after hearing all these ideas I pick and choose the quilting designs I like best.

I decided in this book that I would love to have each of my sisters, sister-in-law, daughters, and daughter-in-law make a project from this book and add their own flair to it. They could change rotation, placement of the block, and could resize the block. They also could add sashing or spacer blocks between the blocks. So in the following pages you will find the creativity of what each of the women has made.

INTRODUCTION

One of the inspirations of this book came from a quilt my mother worked on at one of our family sewing retreats. This pattern is similar to that of *Zig and Zag* (page 17).

She inserted a 1¼" black strip into a fabric square that she had sliced in half at an angle. After she sewed the strip into the square, she trimmed the block to make it into a square again. At some point, I realized that if she had added a 1" strip instead of a 1¼" strip, the block would not need to be trimmed down after she inserted the strip. After realizing this, I thought of all the blocks that I could use with this slicing technique, and it opened up a whole world of ideas.

The concept of this quilt book is based on this very simple idea: the quilts are made with squares, right-angle triangles, 60° diamonds, or odd shapes. The shape is sliced and a 1" strip is inserted, resulting in blocks that can be used in many ways.

How does the pieced block stay the same size? This seems impossible but what happens is ½" of the inserted strip is taken up in the two seams sewn from the strip piece and ½" is taken from the two seams in the original fabric shape, so now you are back to the original size!

Mother and I holding her pieced quilt
Photo by Julia Graber

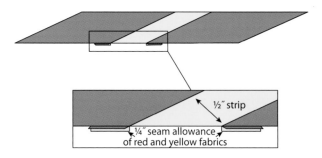

Slice up any block, add a 1" strip, and the block stays the same size! All the quilts featured in this book use just four shapes. Sometimes the strips that are sewn back into the shape will be one color and other times the strips will be many different colors—changing the strip colors adds variations to the overall look of the quilt.

At the beginning of each project there is a picture of the original shape, where it is sliced, and what the shape looks like after the 1" strip is sewn into position.

Each quilt project also has a second quilt in which the block is either resized, has sashing, or has added inset blocks. You'll also see color options to give you more ideas.

GETTING STARTED

SUPPLIES

- Rotary cutter with a sharp new blade

- Rotary cutting mat, 24″ × 36″

- Rotary cutting rulers, 6″ × 24″ and 4″ × 14″ (The smaller ruler is easier to handle when slicing the blocks.)

- Template plastic (*optional*)

- Pins

- Sewing thread to match fabric

- ¼″-wide presser foot (Accurate seam allowances are a must.)

- Scissors

- Seam ripper

- Double-sided tape

- Iron and ironing board

Cutting 60° Diamonds

With this cutting method, equilateral diamonds are cut individually from a fabric strip and then the diamonds will be pieced into a block. An equilateral diamond is created when the strip width is the same as the diamond width in the cutting instructions. This cutting method is used in *Pollygon Patchwork* (page 42). The instructions for each project will indicate the specific strip width and the diamond width.

Here's how to cut the diamonds:

1. For all the diamonds in this book, your cuts will be a 60° angle. Cut the strip width according to your project instructions. This example shows a diamond cut at a 60° angle from a 6½″ strip. Place the strip parallel to the bottom edge of the cutting mat, lining up the edge on a horizontal grid line. Place the ruler on top of the fabric, aligning the ruler's 60° line with the bottom edge of the cut strip. Cut along the right side of the ruler. This initial cut will create the first edge of the diamond.

2. Refer to the project instructions for the desired diamond width. Use a ruler to measure *the width from the first cut edge*, keeping the ruler at the same 60° angle. Make the next cut. Repeat along the length of the strip to make the number of cuts required for the project. This example uses a 6½″-wide ruler to cut the 6½″-wide diamond.

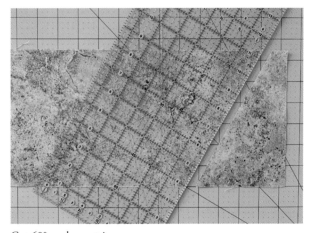

Cut 60° angle on strip.

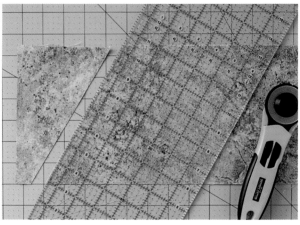

Cut diamond.

Slicing

Each block is sliced, stitched, pressed, trimmed, and stitched again. Only one project has the block cut after the 1″ strip is added into the strip set: *Twilight Table Runner* (page 51).

Two methods are used in this book to slice blocks:

• Slicing with a ruler

• Slicing with a template

SLICING WITH A RULER

Use this method when the project instructions provide specific measurements.

Slice

Slice the shape using the provided measurement(s), in this case, in half.

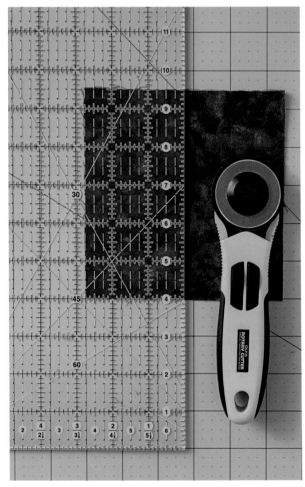

Slice square in half.

Stitch and Press

1. Center a 1″ strip on one of the long sides of the sliced shape. The 1″ strip will always be longer then the shape.

2. Sew the strip in position.

3. Press toward the darker fabric or as instructed in the project.

Trim

Use a ruler and trim the edges of the strip even with the sliced shape. Make sure the ruler is squared up with the shape.

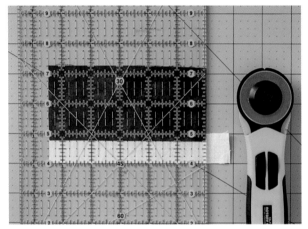

Trim off ends of 1″ strip.

Stitch and Press

1. Sew the other half of the shape to the strip.

2. Press. The block is finished and is back to the original size.

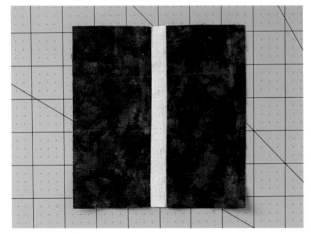

Finished block

SLICING WITH A TEMPLATE

Use this method when the project instructions provide a pattern to make a template.

Template Preparation

The following example uses Just a Square *pattern (page 13). The size of the block is 5½" × 5½" square.*

1. Make a copy of the pattern to trace on plain paper or template plastic. Cut out the template roughly ¼" beyond the outside of the shape.

2. Use a rotary cutter and ruler to cut on the lines of the template, aligning the ¼" ruler line with the seamline on the paper template.

3. Use double-sided tape to secure the template to the underside of a ruler with the slicing edge along the edge of the ruler. If the template has 2 slicing edges, you may want to make 2 templates and tape each to its own ruler. Otherwise, you will have to reposition the single template on the ruler to slice the second side.

Slice

1. Place the ruler on top of a square (or a triangle or diamond shape in a particular project) with the template aligned with one of the corners of the shape. Slice the shape as shown.

> **TIP**
>
> I use paper to make the templates to be taped to the underside of the ruler. If a template will be cut around, then I use plastic for the template, like in *Twilight Table Runner* (page 51).

2. If the template has 2 slicing edges, then position the template on the underside of the ruler and make the first slice. Then reposition the template on the ruler to make the second slice.

Cut along edge of ruler.

Stitch and Press

1. Center a 1" strip to the sliced shape. The 1" strip will always be longer then the shape.

2. Sew the strip in position.

3. Press toward the darker fabric or as instructed in the project.

Trim

Use a ruler and trim the edges of the strip even with the sliced shape. Make sure the ruler is squared up with the shape.

Stitch and Press

1. Sew the other section of the shape to the strip, centering the shape on the strip/shape unit.

2. Press. The shape is finished and is back to the original size.

Piecing a Hexagon

There are three quilts in this book that are hexagon layouts: *Starry Quarry* (page 38), *Pollygon Patchwork* (page 42), and *Twilight Table Runner* (page 51). These diamond blocks require a Y-seam to make a hexagon. A Y-seam is when three pieces of fabric come together at the same point. This point must be marked exactly with a dot ¼″ from the cut edges of each fabric section.

1. Arrange the 3 diamonds needed for sewing a hexagon. With a fabric marker, on the wrong side of the fabric, mark dots ¼″ in from the cut edges of each fabric section. This is where the center of the Y-seam will meet on each of the diamond pieces. You could create your own template to use as a guide in marking the dots. Marking the dots accurately is crucial for the piece to be successful.

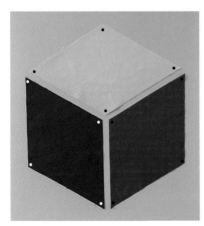
Mark dots precisely.

2. Flip the red diamond onto the blue diamond right sides together.

Place a pin through the matching dots on the red and blue pieces. Start sewing at the pin at the dot. Tack with 3 small stitches. Then continue sewing to the end of the fabric.

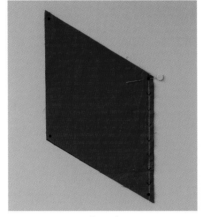
Start sewing exactly at dot.

3. Open the pieces and press the seam toward the red piece.

4. Flip the yellow diamond onto the red diamond. Pin through the matching dots. Make sure all the seams are out of the way, so you will be sewing through only 2 layers of fabric. Start sewing at the dot. Tack with 3 small stitches and then continue to the end of the fabric.

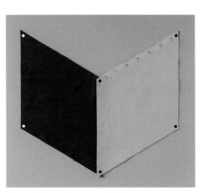
Sew yellow piece to red piece.

5. Open the pieces and press the seam toward the yellow piece. Now you are ready to sew the last leg of the Y-seam. Fold the unit in half, with the right sides of the yellow and blue pieces together. Make sure all the seams are out of the way to sew through only 2 layers of fabric. Start sewing at the dot. Tack with 3 small stitches. Then continue sewing to the end of the fabric.

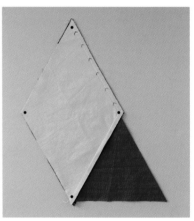
Secure stitches at dot.

6. Open the piece and press the seam toward the blue piece. From the back of the piece, all the seams should be pressed clockwise.

Press seams clockwise.

Joining Hexagon Rows and Columns

Instructions in a project with hexagons will tell you to join the hexagons into rows or columns. It doesn't matter whether it's rows or columns; these steps show you how to join them. For simplicity's sake, these steps refer to columns. Join the hexagon columns by stitching one segment of the seam at a time. At the end of the segment, stop with the needle down, and realign the edges of the hexagons, pivoting to sew the next segment of the seam. Reducing the stitch length will make it easier to stop right on the dot.

1. With the hexagons sewn into columns and the seams pressed open, mark dots on the inside and outside corners of the hexagons on the wrong side of the fabric. These will be your pivot points when stitching the seam. To mark dots, refer to the *Pollygon Patchwork* pattern (page 59).

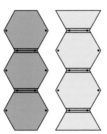

Mark dots at inside and outside hexagon points.

2. Place right sides together with column 2 on top of column 1. Use a pin to match dots. Align the raw edges as shown, and stitch segment 1 from the top edge toward the dot. Remove the pin as you come to the dot and stop with the needle down in the dot. Lift the presser foot to pivot the fabric.

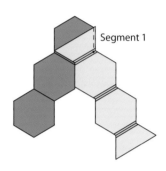

Segment 1

3. As you pivot at the dot, shift column 2 (on top) to the left, while pulling column 1 (underneath) to the right. Smooth out both columns in their new positions and align the fabric edges for segment 2. Pin the next dots together, lower the presser foot, and stitch segment 2.

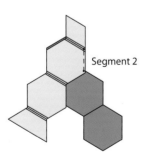

Segment 2

4. When you pivot at the next dot, shift column 2 (on top) to the right, while pulling column 1 (underneath) to the left. Pin the next dots together, lower the presser foot, and stitch segment 3. Continue this process to finish the seam. Press the seam open.

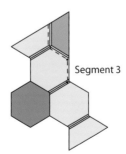

Segment 3

JUST A SQUARE
FINISHED BLOCK: 5″ × 5″ • **FINISHED QUILT:** 40″ × 50″

This is a great project for scraps. When I chose the fabrics for this quilt I went to my scrap box that had precut 5½″ × 5½″ squares. From this box I chose the red and blue squares that had roughly the same values. The squares in this project have two diagonal corners sliced off and the 1″ strip is sewn into these slices. The color placement alternates red and blue squares. My sister's version of this quilt (*Four Square*, page 16) places the colors in larger groups.

Yardage is based on 42″-wide fabric.

Reds: 6 different fabrics, ⅓ yard each

Blues: 6 different fabrics, ⅓ yard each

White: 1 yard

Binding: ⅜ yard

Backing: 48″ × 58″

Batting: 48″ × 58″

CUTTING

WOF = width of fabric

Reds

- **From each red fabric:**
  Cut 1 strip 5½″ × WOF;
  subcut into 7 squares 5½″ × 5½″.
  (You will have a total of 42 red squares;
  you will need only 40 squares.)

Blues

- **From each blue fabric:**
  Cut 1 strip 5½″ × WOF;
  subcut into 7 squares 5½″ × 5½″.
  (You will have a total of 42 blue squares;
  you will need only 40 squares.)

White

- Cut 32 strips 1″ × WOF;
  subcut into 160 strips 1″ × 7″.

Binding

- Cut 5 strips 2¼″ × WOF.

Construction

Refer to Getting Started (page 8) as needed. Seam allowances are ¼″ unless otherwise noted.

MAKE THE BLOCKS

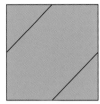 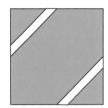

Where to slice the square   Finished block

1. Copy the *Just a Square* pattern (page 58) to make a template. Referring to Slicing with a Template (page 10), use the template taped to the back of a ruler to slice the opposite corners of all the red and blue squares.

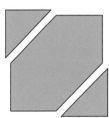

Opposite corners sliced.

2. Sew 2 white 1″ × 7″ strips to each sliced side of the red and blue squares. Press, then trim the ends to match the edges of the block.

3. Center the triangles onto the center unit from Step 2 and sew them into position.

4. Make 40 red blocks and 40 blue blocks.

ASSEMBLE THE QUILT TOP

1. Referring to the quilt layout diagram (next page), arrange the squares accordingly, alternating the red and blue blocks as shown.

2. Sew the blocks into rows. Press the seams in alternate directions from row to row so the seams will nest when you sew the rows together. Then join the rows.

FINISH

Refer to Quiltmaking Basics: How to Finish Your Quilt (page 55) as needed.

Layer, quilt, and bind as desired.

Quilt layout

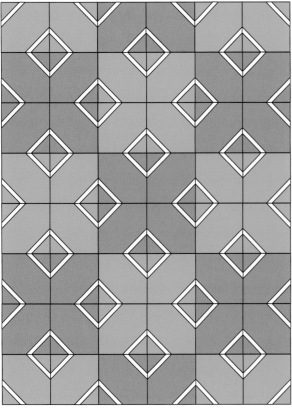

By placing four same-color blocks in a square, you come up with larger block variations.

Four Square by Coleen H. Barnhart, 35″ × 44″, 2016

My sister Coleen made this quilt by using four different colors to make the squares and by placing the colors in diagonal rows.

ZIG AND ZAG

FINISHED BLOCK: 6″ × 6″ • **FINISHED QUILT:** 48″ × 60″

This quilt has a dynamic zigzag going through it as well as a checkerboard background. The border print provide the color scheme for the checkerboard. Notice that the Zig is slanted up hill and the Zag is slanted downhill; so you will need to make two different blocks for this quilt.

MATERIALS

Yardage is based on 42"-wide fabric.

Turquoise: ½ yard

Purple: ½ yard

Blue: ½ yard

Green: ½ yard

Black: 1⅜ yards

Border print: 1⅜ yards

Binding: ½ yard

Backing: 56" × 68"

Batting: 56" × 68"

CUTTING

WOF = width of fabric

Turquoise

• Cut 1 strip 6½" × WOF; subcut into 6 squares 6½" × 6½".

• Cut 2 strips 1" × WOF; subcut into 6 rectangles 1" × 10".

Purple

• Cut 1 strip 6½" × WOF; subcut into 6 squares 6½" × 6½".

• Cut 2 strips 1" × WOF; subcut into 6 rectangles 1" × 10".

Blue

• Cut 1 strip 6½" × WOF; subcut into 6 squares 6½" × 6½".

• Cut 2 strips 1" × WOF; subcut into 6 rectangles 1" × 10".

Green

• Cut 1 strip 6½" × WOF; subcut into 6 squares 6½" × 6½".

• Cut 2 strips 1" × WOF; subcut into 6 rectangles 1" × 10".

Black

• Cut 4 strips 6½" × WOF; subcut into 24 squares 6½" × 6½".

• Cut 14 strips 1" × WOF; subcut into 56 rectangles 1" × 10".

Border print

• Cut 6 strips 6½" × WOF; subcut into 32 squares 6½" × 6½".

• Cut 2 strips 1" × WOF; subcut into 6 strips 1" × 10".

Binding

• Cut into 6 strips 2¼" × WOF.

Construction

Refer to Getting Started (page 8) as needed.

Seam allowances are ¼" unless otherwise noted.

MAKE THE BLOCKS

 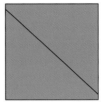

Where to slice the squares

Finished Zig block   Finished Zag block

1. Make a stack of squares for each color. Divide each color stack in half.

2. Copy the *Zig* pattern and the *Zag* pattern (pages 58 and 59). Make a template for each pattern, marking them appropriately. (The patterns are deceptively similar, but each is distinct.)

3. Referring to Slicing with a Template (page 10), tape the Zig template to the underside of a ruler. With the right side of the fabric up, use the ruler and a rotary cutter to slice one stack of each color of squares. Label these Zig stacks.

Zig slices

4. Use Zag template taped to the underside of a ruler to slice the remaining stacks of squares of each color with the right side of the fabric up. Label these Zag stacks.

Zag slices

5. Center a random color 1″ × 10″ strip on one side of a sliced black square and sew in place. Press the seam toward the black. Trim the ends to match the edges of the square.

6. Sew the remainder of the sliced black square to the unit from Step 5 and press.

7. Repeat Steps 5 and 6 to make a total of 12 black Zig blocks and 12 black Zag blocks.

8. Repeat Steps 5 and 6, using black 1″ × 10″ strips with all the sliced border print squares. You will have 16 border print Zig blocks and 16 border print Zag blocks.

9. Repeat Steps 5 and 6, using black 1″ × 10″ strips with all the sliced turquoise, purple, blue, and green sliced squares. You will have 3 Zig blocks and 3 Zag blocks of each color.

ASSEMBLE THE QUILT TOP

1. Referring to the quilt layout diagram (below), arrange the blocks to form a checkerboard in the center and the 32 print blocks as the border. Keep in mind you have Zig blocks and Zag blocks that create the zigzag.

2. Sew the blocks into rows. Press the seams in alternate directions from row to row so the seams nest when you sew together the rows. Then join the rows.

FINISH

Refer to Quiltmaking Basics: How to Finish Your Quilt (page 55) as needed.

Layer, quilt, and bind as desired.

Quilt layout

This quilt is different from the project because strips are the same color and blocks in every other row are rotated 180°. Instead of a chevron, a diamond-shape design is formed across the quilt.

Sew Simple by Melissa Cline, 54″ × 63″, 2016

My daughter-in-law Melissa made this quilt by using the same fabric in each row.

THROUGH THE LATTICE

FINISHED BLOCK: 9½″ × 9½″ • **FINISHED QUILT:** 47″ × 56½″

The border of this quilt is created by using one color of blocks around the quilt. The X in the border block is still the same color as the X in the rest of the quilt blocks, so the design continues into the borders. I have chosen a dark fabric for the X so it will contrast with the rainbow colors in the blocks. This helps to create an illusion of depth that there is a lattice over the quilt squares.

Yardage is based on 42"-wide fabric.

Pinks: 2 different fabrics, ⅓ yard each

Oranges: 2 different fabrics, ⅓ yard each

Yellows: 2 different fabrics, ⅓ yard each

Greens: 2 different fabrics, ⅓ yard each

Blues: 2 different fabrics, ⅓ yard each

Border print: 1¼ yards

Navy: 1 yard

Binding: ½ yard

Backing: 55" × 65"

Batting: 55" × 65"

CUTTING

WOF = width of fabric

Pinks, oranges, yellows, greens, and blues

• **From each fabric:**
  Cut 1 strip 10" × WOF;
  subcut into 2 squares 10" × 10".
  (You will have a total of 4 pink, 4 orange, 4 yellow, 4 green, and 4 blue squares.)

Border print

• Cut 3 strips 10" × WOF;
  subcut into 10 squares 10" × 10".

Navy

• Cut 15 strips 1" × WOF;
  subcut into 60 rectangles 1" × 8½".

• Cut 15 strips 1" × WOF;
  subcut into 30 rectangles 1" × 16".

Binding

• Cut 6 strips 2¼" × WOF.

Construction

Refer to Getting Started (page 8) as needed.

Seam allowances are ¼" unless otherwise noted.

MAKE THE BLOCKS

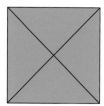 

Where to slice the squares

Finished block

1. Referring to Slicing with a Ruler (page 9), slice all the 10" × 10" squares twice on the diagonal.

TIP

It is important to keep each sliced block with its other quarters. If there is a design in the fabric it keeps the fabric design placements together and keeps the design in the correct orientation.

2. Center a navy 1" × 8½" strip between 2 adjacent triangles of a sliced square and sew the strip into place. Press the seams toward the triangles. Trim the strip even with block edges.

Repeat with the 2 remaining adjacent triangles.

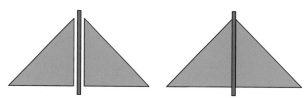

Sew strip between adjacent triangles.

3. Trim the strips even with the triangle edges, creating 90° corners.

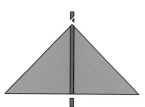

Trim strips even with triangle edges.

4. Center and sew a navy 1″ × 16″ strip between the 2 units from Step 3. Press the seams toward the triangles. Trim the strip even with the triangle edges, creating 90° corners.

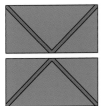

Sew center strip into block and trim.

5. Repeat Steps 2–4 with all the diagonally cut 10″ × 10″ squares.

6. Cut 9 border print blocks in half from side to side.

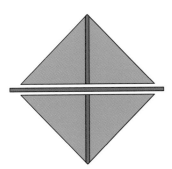

Border half-blocks

7. Cut remaining border print block into quarters from side to side. These 4 quarters will be used for the corner squares in the border.

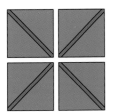

Border print quarter-block

ASSEMBLE THE QUILT TOP

1. Referring to the quilt layout diagram (below), arrange the center blocks as shown. Then add the border print half and quarter blocks as the border. Keep the X design continuing into the borders.

2. Sew the blocks into rows. Press the seams in alternate directions from row to row and then join the rows.

FINISH

Refer to Quiltmaking Basics: How to Finish Your Quilt (page 55) as needed.

Layer, quilt, and bind as desired.

Quilt layout

Every other block is a white block with a color strip inserted; all color blocks have a white strip inserted.

Railroad Crossing by June Flory, 46″ × 35″, 2016

My sister June made this variation, combining large- and small-pieced blocks with some small solid squares. She also added sashing between the blocks, allowing some of the X's to float.

ZEBRA IN THE NURSERY
FINISHED BLOCK: 7″ × 7″ • **FINISHED QUILT:** 35″ × 49″

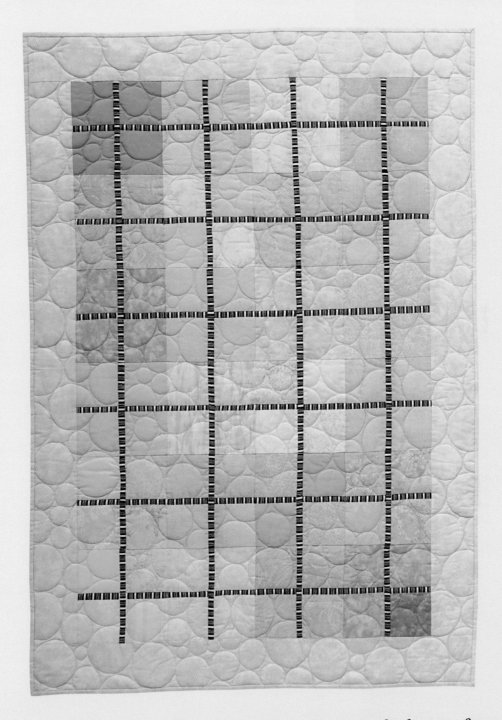

A quick baby quilt with pastel colors will warm the heart of any mother who has just had a little one. The stripe fabric in each square gives the quilt a modern element, and the circles of different sizes quilted throughout the quilt add a warm bubbly feel.

MATERIALS

Yardage is based on 42"-wide fabric.

Pastels: 12–24 different fabrics, ¼ yard each

Stripes: ½ yard

Light turquoise: ⅝ yard

Binding: ½ yard

Backing: 43" × 57"

Batting: 43" × 57"

CUTTING

WOF = width of fabric

Pastels

• **From each fabric:** Cut 1–2 squares 7½" × 7½" for a total of 24 pastel squares.

Stripes

• Cut 6 strips 1" × WOF; subcut into 48 strips 1" × 5".

• Cut 6 strips 1" × WOF; subcut into 24 strips 1" × 8½".

Light turquoise

• Cut 4 strips 4" × WOF.

Binding

• Cut 5 strips 2¼" × WOF.

Construction

Refer to Getting Started (page 8) as needed.
Seam allowances are ¼" unless otherwise noted.

MAKE THE BLOCKS

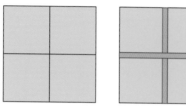

Where to slice the squares   Finished block

1. Referring to Slicing with a Ruler (page 9), cut all the blocks in half horizontally at the 3¾" line using the ruler. Without moving the sliced block cut the block again vertically at the 3¾" line.

TIP

It is important to keep each sliced block with its other quarters. If there is a design in the fabric it keeps the fabric design placements together and keeps the design in the correct orientation.

2. Center and sew a 1" × 5" strip between the top 2 quarters of a sliced square. Center and sew another 1" × 5" between the bottom 2 quarters of the sliced square. Trim the edges even with block edges.

Sew strip between quarters of sliced block.

3. Center and sew the 1" × 8½" between these the units from Step 2. Trim the edges even with the block edges.

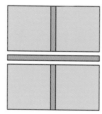

Sew block together.

ASSEMBLE THE QUILT TOP

1. Referring to the quilt layout diagram (below), arrange the blocks for the quilt center.

2. Sew the blocks into rows. Press the seams in alternate directions from row to row. Then join the rows.

3. Sew the light turquoise 4″ × WOF strips together end-to end. Cut 2 strips 4″ × 42½″. Sew these to the sides of the quilt.

4. From the remaining pieced border strip, cut 2 strips 4″ × 35½″. Sew these to the top and bottom of the quilt.

FINISH

Refer to Quiltmaking Basics: How to Finish Your Quilt (page 55) as needed.

Layer, quilt, and bind as desired.

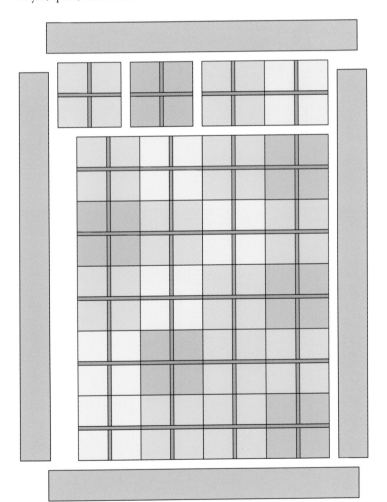

Quilt layout

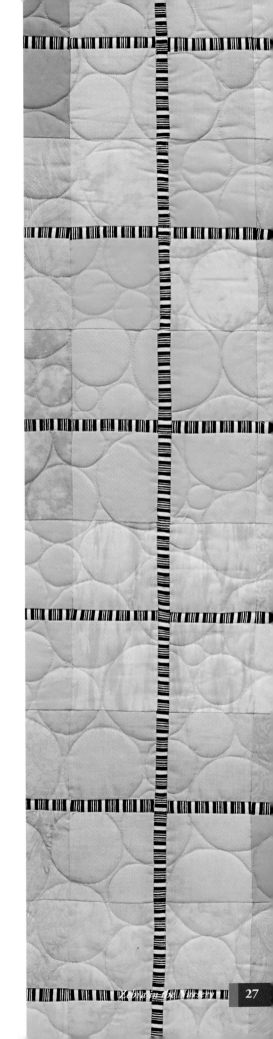

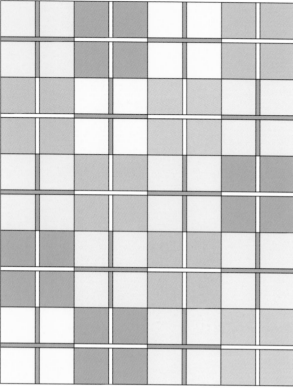

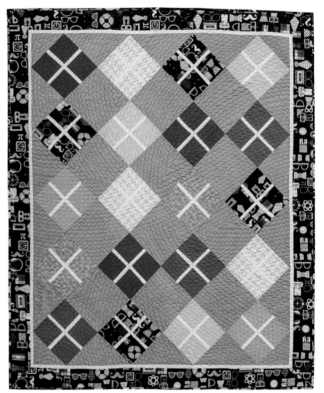

Shades of blues create a one-color quilt. Dark blue squares have light blue strips, and light blue strips have dark blue strips.

Packages for George by Sheila Helmuth, 46″ × 56″, 2016

Sheila's variation has the blocks on-point with a solid block between each sliced block for a bit larger and quicker rendition of *Zebra in the Nursery*.

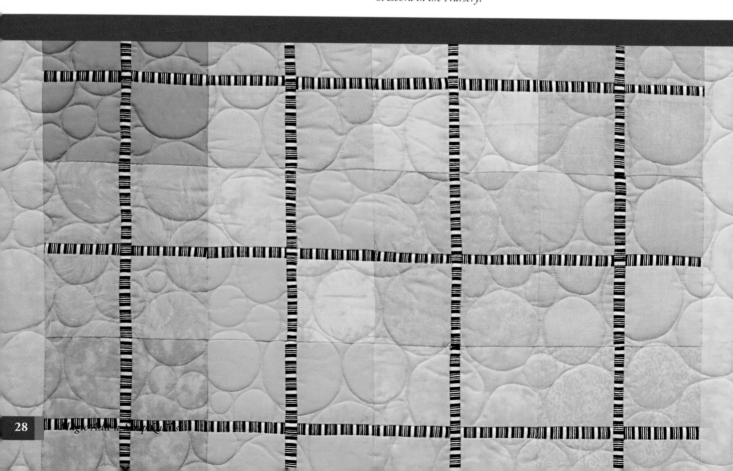

UP AND DOWN THE STEPS

FINISHED BLOCK: 8″ × 8″ • **FINISHED QUILT:** 61″ × 77″

This is a three-color quilt. From each colorway, you'll need four fabrics in different values. Fabric squares are cut once into two triangles, and then the triangles are sliced and pieced with a variegated striped fabric. Two pieced triangles are joined to make a block. By turning and positioning the blocks, this quilt has the illusion of overlapping large squares. For the strips, I chose a variegated stripe fabric that has many colors and selected the colors for the blocks based on the colors of the stripes.

Yardage is based on 42"-wide fabric.

Dark brown: 1½ yards

Medium brown: ⅞ yard

Medium/light brown: ⅞ yard

Light brown: ⅝ yard

Dark blue: ⅞ yard

Medium blue: ⅝ yard

Medium/light blue: ⅞ yard

Light blue: ⅞ yard

Dark green: ⅞ yard

Medium green: ⅝ yard

Medium/light green: ⅞ yard

Light green: ⅞ yard

Stripes: 1¾ yards

Binding: ⅝ yard

Backing: 69" × 85"

Batting: 69" × 85"

CUTTING

WOF = width of fabric

Dark brown

• Cut 2 strips 9" × WOF;
  subcut into 6 squares 9" × 9".

• Cut 7 strips 2½" × WOF
  for the outer border.

Medium brown

• Cut 2 strips 9" × WOF;
  subcut into 7 squares 9" × 9".

Medium/light brown

• Cut 2 strips 9" × WOF;
  subcut into 5 squares 9" × 9".

Light brown

• Cut 1 strip 9" × WOF;
  subcut into 3 squares 9" × 9".

Dark blue

• Cut 2 strips 9" × WOF;
  subcut into 6 squares 9" × 9".

Medium blue

• Cut 1 strip 9" × WOF;
  subcut into 3 squares 9" × 9".

Medium/light blue

• Cut 2 strips 9" × WOF;
  subcut into 6 squares 9" × 9".

Light blue

• Cut 2 strips 9" × WOF;
  subcut into 6 squares 9" × 9".

Dark green

• Cut 2 strips 9" × WOF;
  subcut into 6 squares 9" × 9".

Medium green

• Cut 1 strip 9" × WOF;
  subcut into 4 squares 9" × 9".

Medium/light green

• Cut 2 strips 9" × WOF;
  subcut into 6 squares 9" × 9".

Light green

• Cut 2 strips 9" × WOF;
  subcut into 5 squares 9" × 9".

Stripes

• Cut 18 strips 1" × WOF;
  subcut into 126 strips 1" × 5½".

• Cut 32 strips 1" × WOF;
  subcut into 126 strips 1" × 8½".

• Cut 7 strips 1" × WOF
  for the inner border.

Binding

• Cut 8 strips 2¼" × WOF.

Construction

Refer to Getting Started (page 8) as needed. Seam allowances are ¼" unless otherwise noted.

MAKE THE BLOCKS

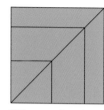

Where to slice the squares 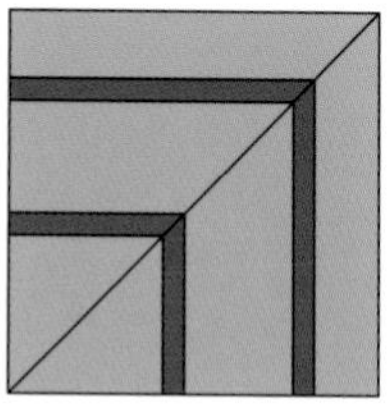   Finished block

1. Referring to Slicing with a Ruler (page 9), slice all the 9" × 9" squares diagonally once into 2 triangles.

TIP

Keep each sliced block together. If there is a design in the fabric it keeps the fabric design placements together and keeps the design in the correct orientation.

2. Position 2 triangles from 1 square as shown. Keeping the triangles in this position, use a ruler to make 2 slices in each triangle, measuring from the edges of each triangle as exactly shown.

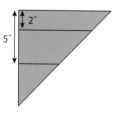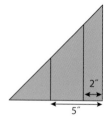

Keeping each triangle positioned as shown, measure and slice as indicated.

3. Sew the stripe 1″ × 8½″ strips into the 2″ slices and sew the stripe 1″ × 5½″ strips into the 5″ slices. Trim the strips even with the triangles.

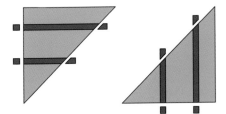

Sew strips into triangles.

4. Sew together the pairs of triangles to make a block. Trim the block to 8½″ × 8½″ if needed.

ASSEMBLE THE QUILT TOP

1. Referring to the quilt layout diagram, arrange the blocks in 9 rows with 7 blocks in each row for the quilt center.

2. Sew the blocks into rows. Press the seams in alternate directions from row to row so the seams nest when you sew together the rows. Join the rows.

3. For the inner border, sew the striped 1″ × WOF strips together end to end. Cut 2 strips 1″ × 72½″. Sew these to the sides of the quilt center.

4. From the remaining striped strip, cut 2 strips 1″ × 57½″. Sew these to the top and bottom of the quilt center.

5. For the outer border, sew the dark brown 2½″ × WOF strips together end to end. Cut 2 strips 2½″ × 73½″ and sew these to the side of the quilt.

6. From the remaining dark brown strip, cut 2 strips 2½″ × 61½″. Sew these to the top and bottom of the quilt.

FINISH

Refer to Quiltmaking Basics: How to Finish Your Quilt (page 55) as needed.

Layer, quilt, and bind as desired.

Quilt layout

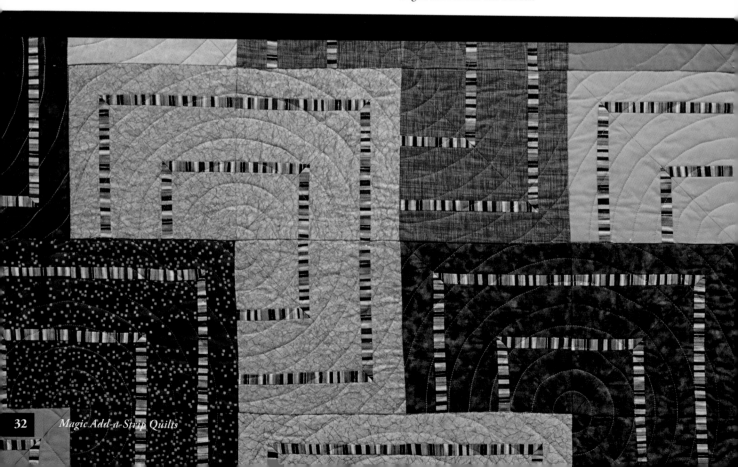

Rotating triangle blocks creates a focus on the center of the quilt instead of stairs.

Red Box by Emily Hostetler, 80″ × 88½, 2016

Emily, my sixth sister, chose fabrics of reds, tans and creams. She rotated her triangle blocks and made her squares go in many directions. She also let the triangles extend into the border.

COMPASS

FINISHED BLOCK: 9″ × 9″ • **FINISHED QUILT:** 54″ × 72″

Compass is made up of red fabrics in dark values and gray fabrics in lighter values. The triangle block is a half-square triangle, which means that two triangles pieced together will make a square. In this project, after you slice the triangle you match a red star point with a gray background to make a triangle unit and you match a gray star point to a red background to make a triangle unit. These two units are sewn together to make a square.

Yardage is based on 42″-wide fabric.

Reds: 6 different fabrics, ⅝ yard each

Grays: 6 different fabrics, ⅝ yard each

Black: 1¼ yards

Binding: ¾ yard

Backing: 62″ × 80″

Batting: 62″ × 80″

CUTTING

WOF = width of fabric

Reds

• **From each fabric:**
  Cut 1 strip 10″ × WOF;
  subcut into 4 squares 10″ × 10″.
  (You will have a total of 24 red squares.)

Grays

• **From each fabric:**
  Cut 1 strip 10″ × WOF;
  subcut into 4 squares 10″ × 10″.
  (You will have a total of 24 gray squares.)

Black

• Cut 39 strips 1″ × WOF;
  subcut into 192 strips 1″ × 7½″.

Binding

• Cut 7 strips 2¼″ × WOF.

Construction

Refer to Getting Started (page 8) as needed. Seam allowances are ¼″ unless otherwise noted.

MAKE THE BLOCKS

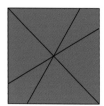 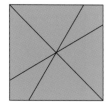 

Where to slice the squares   Finished block

1. Referring to Slicing with a Ruler (page 9), slice all the red and gray 10″ × 10″ squares once diagonally. You will have 48 red and 48 gray right triangles.

2. Referring to Slicing with a Template (page 10), copy the *Compass* pattern (page 58) and make a template of plain paper.

3. When taping the paper template to the underside of the ruler, match the ¼″ line on the ruler with the ¼″ line on the template and align the template with the edge of the ruler. Working with only 1 red triangle and 1 gray triangle, slice the triangles with the ruler and a rotary cutter. You will slice along one side of the template and then you will need to

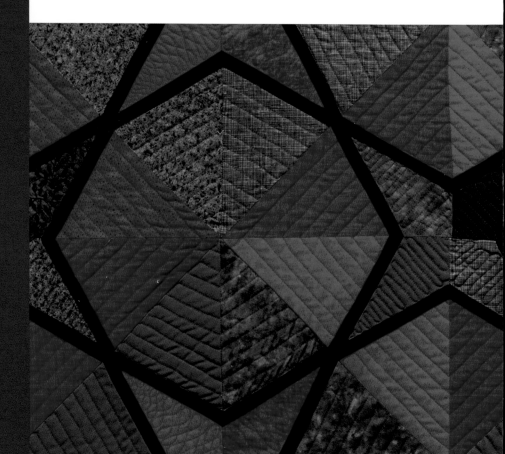

reposition the template on the ruler to cut the second template edge. Be very careful to keep the same orientation of the resulting pieces. (Do not cut all the red and gray triangles now. It is too difficult to keep them all in the proper orientation after cutting.)

* Attention! *

It is critical before slicing the triangle that the right angle of the template matches exactly with the right angle of the triangle. This places the tip of the template in the center of the long (hypotenuse) side of the triangle for the correct position to slice the piece.

4. With the red and gray triangles pieces in their proper orientation from Step 3, trade the center sections so you have a gray point with red sides and a red point with gray sides.

Trade center points.

5. You will sew black 1″ × 7½″ strips into the slices of each triangle. Center and sew a 1″ × 7½″ strip onto a sidepiece. Press the seam open and trim the strip to match the edges of the triangle sidepiece.

6. Center and sew another black 1″ × 7½″ strip to the other sidepiece. Press the seams open and trim the ends to match the edges of the triangle sidepiece.

7. Sew the sidepieces to the star points, pressing each seam open. Repeat Steps 3–7 to make 48 units of each color combination.

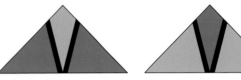

Make 48 of each.

8. Select 2 opposite color combination units from Step 7 to sew together to make a block. Press the seam open. Repeat to make a total of 48 blocks.

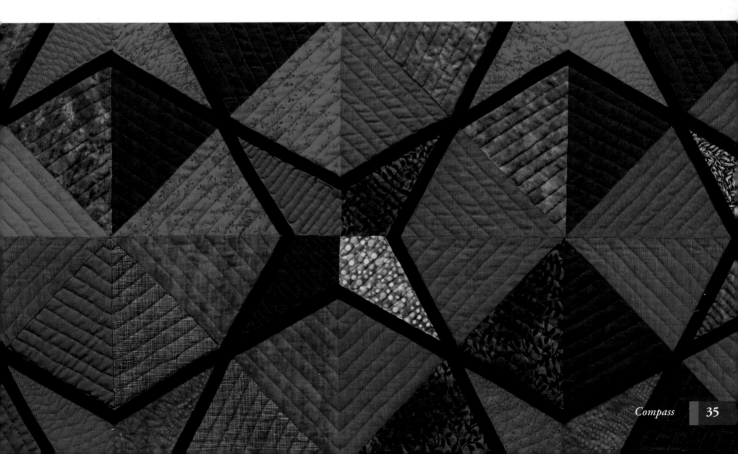

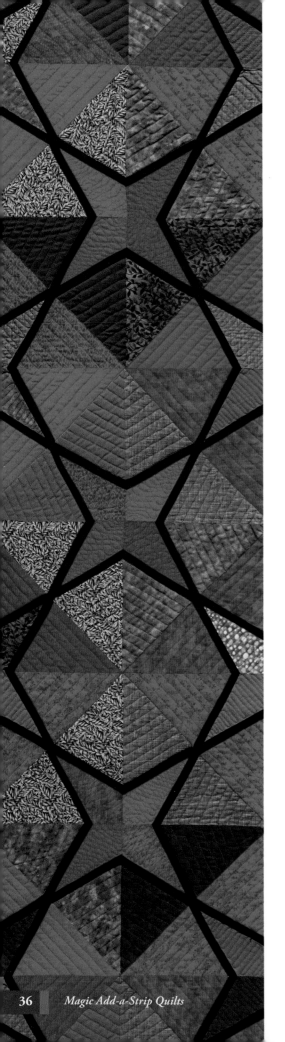

ASSEMBLE THE QUILT TOP

1. Referring to the quilt layout diagram (below), arrange the blocks 8 rows with 6 blocks in each row.

2. Sew the blocks into rows. Press the seams in alternate directions from row to row so the seams nest when you sew together the rows. Join the rows.

FINISH

Refer to Quiltmaking Basics: How to Finish Your Quilt (page 55) as needed.

Layer, quilt, and bind as desired.

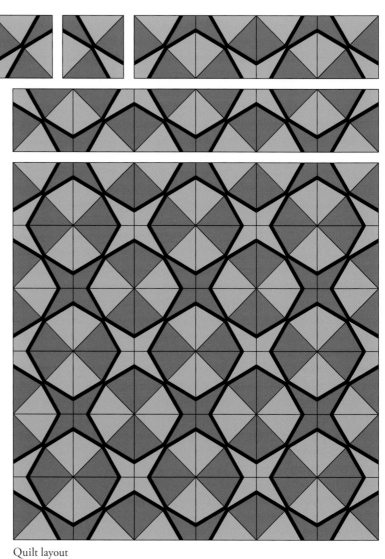

Quilt layout

COLOR OPTIONS AND VARIATIONS

Blue and yellow in the modern RGB additive color model is one of the complementary pairs.

This creates a pleasing to the eye combination of color.

Blue and yellow

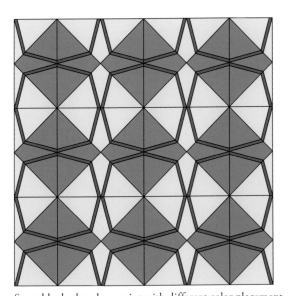

Same block placed on-point with different color placement.

Ruby Stained Glass by Julia H. Graber, 54″ × 72″, 2016

When my sister Julia made this quilt, she changed the colors of the blocks around the outside of the quilt to create the border.

STARRY QUARRY

FINISHED QUILT: 90″ × 102″

Designed and made by Autumn Sensenig

For the stars in this quilt there are eleven different light and dark fabric combinations in the star points. With the dark value on one side of the diamond, a pinwheel appears, and if you turn the diamond around, a star will appear. Magic!

Yardage is based on 42"-wide fabric.

Star fabrics: 11 light fabrics and 11 dark fabrics, ⅔ yard each (pairing a light/dark set of fabrics as you select them)

Cream: 4¾ yards

Dark brown: 1½ yards

Binding: ⅞ yard

Backing: 98" × 110"

Batting: 98" × 110"

CUTTING

Refer to Cutting 60° Diamonds (page 8). • WOF = width of fabric

Star fabrics

From each fabric set (keeping the diamonds from each set together):

• Cut 2 light strips 6½" × WOF; subcut into 6 diamonds 6½" × 6½".

• Cut 2 dark strips 6½" × WOF; subcut into 6 diamonds 6½" × 6½".

(You will have a total of 66 light and 66 dark diamonds.)

Cream

• Cut 18 strips 6½" × WOF; subcut into 71 diamonds 6½" × 6½".

• Cut 1 strip 7¼" × WOF; subcut into 4 diamonds 7¼" × 7¼".

• Cut 11 strips 3½" × WOF.

Dark brown

• Cut 44 strips 1" × WOF; subcut into 132 strips 1" × 13".

Binding

• Cut 11 strips 2¼" × WOF.

Construction

Refer to Getting Started (page 8) as needed. Seam allowances are ¼" unless otherwise noted.

MAKE THE BLOCKS

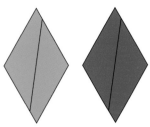

Where to slice the diamond

Finished diamonds

1. Referring to Slicing with a Template (page 10), copy the *Starry Quarry* pattern (page 60) to make a template. Be sure to mark the seamlines and the dot on the template. Tape the template to the back of a ruler, aligning the slicing edge on the template with the edge of the ruler. With the fabric right side up, slice all the light/dark sets of diamonds. *Do not slice the cream diamonds.*

2. Within each light/dark sets of diamonds, trade the diamond pieces to create the light/dark diamond combinations.

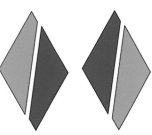

Light/dark diamond combination

3. Center and sew a dark brown 1" × 13" strip to one side of the diamond, then trim to match diamond edges. Center the remaining half of the diamond and sew to complete the diamond.

Stitch diamond.

4. Referring to Slicing with a Ruler (page 9), slice 3 cream 7¼" diamonds horizontally (width) from point to point to make equilateral triangles. Then slice the remaining cream 7¼" diamond into quarters from point to point vertically (length) and horizontally (width).

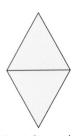 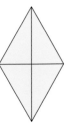

Cut 3 diamonds in half.   Cut 1 diamond into quarters.

ASSEMBLE THE QUILT TOP

1. Referring to the quilt layout diagram (below), arrange the pieced diamonds with 18 complete stars in the center and 4 partial stars on the sides. Then add the cream diamonds, half-diamonds, and corner triangles to the design wall. Using a design wall allows you to step back to check the layout and color balance. You will have 8 extra pieced diamonds, but this allows you more choices for your layout.

2. On the layout diagram, you can see outlines for hexagons. Referring to Piecing a Hexagon (page 11), sew

3 diamonds together to make each hexagon. Press the seams clockwise. Some of the units will be partial hexagons. Replace each unit on the design wall.

3. Sew the hexagons into columns. Press the seams open.

4. Before joining the columns together, sew individual pieced diamonds and cream diamonds to the outside columns of hexagons.

5. Referring to Joining Hexagon Rows and Columns (page 12), sew the columns together. Then trim the

quilt sides by cutting through the length of the diamonds as shown in the quilt layout diagram. Last, add the 4 corner pieces to the quilt.

6. Sew the cream 3½″ × WOF strips together end to end. Cut 2 strips 3½″ × 96½″. Sew these to the sides of the quilt.

7. Cut 2 cream 3½″ × 90½″ strips. Sew these to the top and bottom of the quilt.

FINISH

Refer to Quiltmaking Basics: How to Finish Your Quilt (page 55) as needed.

Layer, quilt, and bind as desired.

Quilt layout

This quilt variation uses green and gray fabrics. The red used in strips give quilt flair, and black background enhances stars. Occasional yellow adds unexpected pop.

In the Wind by Barbara Cline, 51½″ × 74″, 2016

In this quilt no background blocks circle around stars, so when diamond blocks come together, the design creates interlocking pinwheels instead of stars.

POLLYGON PATCHWORK

FINISHED QUILT: 60″ × 69″

Designed and made by Polly Yoder

Polly used thirteen different fabrics in three colorways, with each colorway having a variety of values that create a quilt with character. The oranges add some pop and zip to the mostly navy quilt.

MATERIALS

Yardage is based on 42"-wide fabric.

Oranges: 3 different shades,
⅝ yard each

Greens: 5 different shades,
⅝ yard each

Blues: 5 different shades,
⅝ yard each

Navy: 3⅝ yards

Binding: ⅝ yard

Backing: 68" × 77"

Batting: 68" × 77"

CUTTING

*Refer to Cutting 60° Diamonds
(page 8).* • *WOF = width of fabric*

Oranges, greens, and blues

• **From each fabric:**
Cut 2 strips 5½" × WOF;
subcut into 6 diamonds
5½" × 5½".

• **From each fabric:**
Cut 3 strips 1" × WOF;
subcut into 12 strips 1" × 8".

Navy

• Cut 16 strips 5½" × WOF;
subcut into 78 diamonds
5½" × 5½"

• Cut 32 strips 1" × WOF;
subcut into 156 strips 1" × 8".

Binding

• Cut 7 strips 2¼" × WOF.

Construction

Refer to Getting Started (page 8) as needed.
Seam allowances are ¼" unless otherwise noted.

MAKE THE BLOCKS

Where to slice   Finished
the diamond   diamond

1. Before slicing any diamonds, organize your cut pieces into 13 sets with each set to include 6 matching color diamonds, 12 matching 1" × 8" strips, 6 navy diamonds, and 12 navy 1" × 8" strips. You will slice and sew the sets *one set at a time.*

2. Referring to Slicing with a Template (page 10), copy the *Pollygon Patchwork* pattern (page 59) and make a paper template. Be sure to mark the seamlines and the dots on the template. Tape the template to the underside of a ruler, with the slicing edge along the edge of the ruler. With the right side of the fabric up, use the ruler and a rotary cutter to slice all the diamonds in 1 set from Step 1.

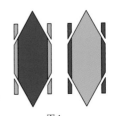

Trim.

3. Center and sew a 1" × 8" strip to one side of the center piece of each diamond. Press and trim the ends to match the edges of the diamond shape.

4. Sew the remaining triangles from Step 2 to the units to complete the diamonds as shown. Press. You will have 6 diamonds pieced with navy strips and 6 navy diamonds pieced with color strips in this set.

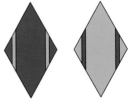

Make 6 of each.

5. Repeat Steps 2–4 with each of the remaining 12 sets from Step 1. You will have a total of 78 diamonds pieced with navy strips and 78 navy diamonds pieced with color strips.

ASSEMBLE THE QUILT TOP

1. Refer to the quilt layout diagram (at right). On a design wall, arrange the diamonds into hexagons and partial hexagons as shown. You will have 2 extra color pieced diamonds.

2. Once all the diamonds are in a pleasing color arrangement, cut the extending diamonds lengthwise along the top and the bottom of the quilt, making long half-diamonds. Do not trim any of the extending diamonds on the sides of the quilt. These will be trimmed in Step 4.

3. Referring to Piecing a Hexagon (page 11), sew 3 diamonds together. Be sure to mark the dots on the sides of the diamonds. You will also sew some partial hexagons together as indicated in the layout. Return the sewn hexagons and partial hexagons to the design wall.

4. Sew the hexagons into rows, pressing the seams open between the hexagons. Return the rows to the design wall.

5. Referring to Joining Hexagon Rows and Columns (page 12), sew the rows together. Trim the extended diamonds on each side of the quilt.

FINISH

Refer to Quiltmaking Basics: How to Finish Your Quilt (page 55) as needed.

Layer, quilt, and bind as desired.

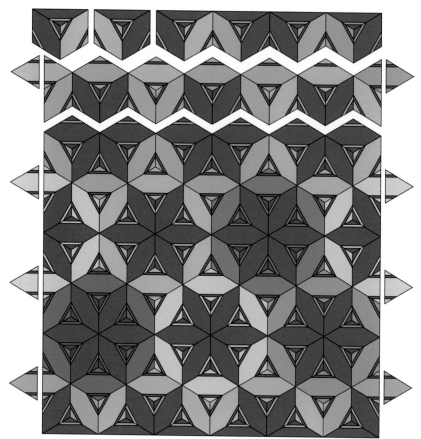

Quilt layout

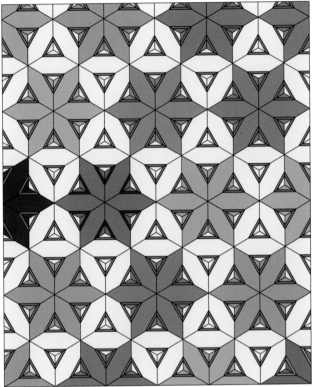

All diamond blocks around stars are gray, making stars instead of hexagons pop out. Splash of red color for strips makes one's eyes focus on triangles instead of hexagons.

Who Spilt the Crayons? by Barbara Cline, 97″ × 97″, 2016

Diamonds in this quilt are 2″ larger in comparison to diamonds in *Pollygon Patchwork* (page 42). Therefore, the 1″ inserted strip is smaller in comparison to diamonds.

ARGYLE

FINISHED QUILT: 67″ × 80″

Each diamond has a diagonal black or white X through it. The few lighter diamonds have a black X, which gives the quilt some zip. The white border is pieced on the sides and is appliquéd at the top and bottom of the quilt, framing the quilt center in very unique angles.

MATERIALS

Yardage is based on 42"-wide fabric.

Coordinating fabrics (17):

• 13 fabrics, ½ yard each

• 4 additional fabrics, ¾ yard each

White: 3 yards

Black: ¼ yard

Fusible web: 1½ yards of lightweight, paper-backed, 20"-wide fusible web

Binding: ⅝ yard

Backing: 75" × 88"

Batting: 75" × 88"

CUTTING

Refer to Cutting 60° Diamonds (page 8).
WOF = width of fabric

Coordinating fabrics

• **From each of 13 fabrics:** Cut 1 strip 7½" × WOF; subcut into 4 diamonds 7½" × 7½".

• **From each of 4 fabrics:** Cut 2 strips 7½" × WOF; subcut into 5 diamonds 7½" × 7½".

White

• Cut 1 piece 9" × WOF. Following manufacturer's instructions, fuse a 8" × 40" piece of fusible web to the strip. Then cut 1 strip 7⅜" × WOF; subcut into 4 diamonds 7⅜" × 7⅜". *Do not remove the paper backing.*

• Cut 2 strips 8" × WOF; subcut into 5 diamonds 8" × 8".

• Cut 7 strips 5½" × WOF.

• Cut 36 strips 1" × WOF; subcut into 66 strips 1" × 10" and 132 strips 1" × 5½".

Black

• Cut 4 strips 1" × WOF; subcut into 6 strips 1" × 10" and 12 strips 1" × 5½".

Binding

• Cut 8 strips 2¼" × WOF.

Construction

Refer to Getting Started (page 8) as needed.
Seam allowances are ¼" unless otherwise noted.

MAKE THE BLOCKS

Where to slice   Finished
the diamond   diamond

1. Referring to Slicing with a Ruler (page 9), slice the 5 white 8" × 8" diamonds in half lengthwise to create 10 long half-diamonds to be used along the quilt sides. Set these aside.

2. Slice the paper-backed diamonds in half lengthwise to create 8 long half-diamonds. Keep the paper backing in place. Set these aside.

3. Using a ruler, slice all the coordinating fabric diamonds in half in both directions by measuring in 3¾" from each side as shown.

Measure and slice at 3¾" in both directions.

TIP

It is important to keep each sliced block with its other quarters. If there is a design in the fabric it keeps the fabric placement together and keeps the design of the fabric flowing.

4. Decide on 6 diamonds you want to accent with the black strips. (I used 6 lighter diamonds.) For each of those diamonds, center and sew a black 1″ × 5½″ strip between 2 adjacent pieces and sew a black 1″ × 5½″ strip between the remaining 2 adjacent pieces as shown. Press and trim the strip ends.

5. Center and sew a black 1″ × 10″ strip between the units from Step 4. Press and trim the strip ends.

6. Repeat Steps 4 and 5 to make a total of 6 diamonds with black strips.

7. Repeat Steps 4 and 5 using the remaining coordinating fabric diamonds, white 1″ × 5½″ strips, and white 1″ × 10″ strips to make a total of 66 diamonds with white strips.

Make
66 diamonds
with white strips.

ASSEMBLE THE QUILT TOP

1. Referring to the quilt layout diagram (next page), arrange the pieced diamonds into diagonal rows. Reserve the 8 paper-backed half-diamonds for later, but add the other 10 white half-diamonds along the sides of the quilt center.

2. Sew the diamonds blocks into diagonal rows. Press the seams in alternate directions from row to row so the seams nest when you sew together the rows. Join the rows.

3. Trim the top and bottom of the quilt center straight across, removing the extended diamond triangles as shown in the layout.

APPLIQUÉ AND BORDER

1. Referring to the quilt photo (page 46), review how the white triangles go across the top and bottom of the quilt center. Position 4 paper-backed white half-diamonds 7⅜″ × 7⅜″ across the bottom of the quilt, as shown, and position the remaining 4 half-diamonds across the top. Fuse the half-diamonds to the quilt center, following the manufacturer's instructions.

Half-diamonds at bottom of quilt center

2. Appliqué the white half-diamonds onto the quilt with white thread using a small zigzag stitch.

TIP

The fabric behind my white half-diamonds showed through the white; so after I appliquéd the half-diamonds, I used my iron to reheat the half-diamonds. Then I carefully trimmed away the fabric behind the white.

3. Sew the white 5½″ strips together end to end. Cut 2 strips 5½″ × 70½″. Sew these to the sides of the quilt.

4. Cut 2 strips 5½″ × 67½″ and sew to the top and bottom of the quilt.

FINISH

Refer to Quiltmaking Basics: How to Finish Your Quilt (page 55) as needed.

Layer, quilt, and bind as desired.

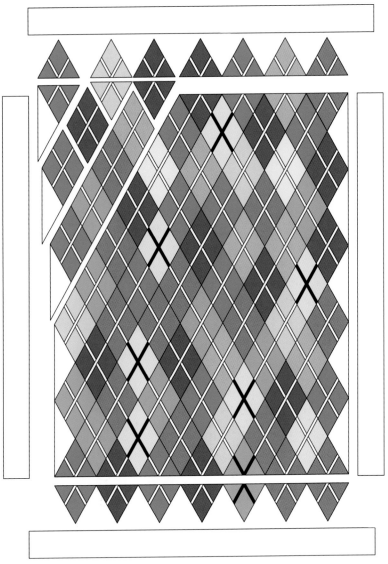

Quilt layout

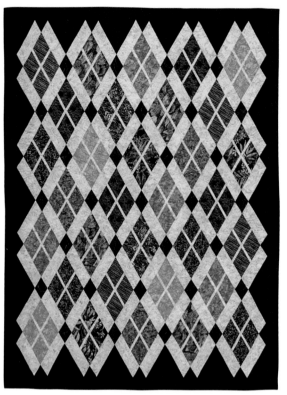

With this color variation, the strips look like a black diamond lattice lying on top of the blocks.

Summer Skies by Cheryl Y. Heatwole, 60″ × 80″, 2016

My sister-in-law Cheryl made this variation with sashing added between the blocks and black cornerstones. Notice how the side of the quilt has half black blocks; the last border is also black, creating floating diamonds along the quilt edges.

For this option, blocks are placed in a baby block layout rather than in rows.

TWILIGHT TABLE RUNNER

FINISHED QUILT: 21″ × 60″

The spinning pinwheels inside the stars give movement to this table runner. Do you see stars or do you see pinwheels? The vivid colors make a great contrast with the black background.

Yardage is based on 42"-wide fabric.

Dark turquoise: ⅝ yard   **Black:** ⅝ yard

Light turquoise: ⅝ yard   **Border print:** ⅝ yard

Dark purple: ⅝ yard   **Binding:** ½ yard

Light purple: ⅝ yard   **Backing:** 29" × 68"

Dark blue: ⅜ yard   **Backing:** 29" × 68"

Light blue: ½ yard

CUTTING

Refer to Cutting 60° Diamonds (page 8).
WOF = width of fabric

Dark turquoise
- Cut 4 strips
  3½" × WOF.

Light turquoise
- Cut 4 strips
  3½" × WOF.

Dark purple
- Cut 4 strips
  3½" × WOF.

Light purple
- Cut 4 strips
  3½" × WOF.

Dark blue
- Cut 2 strips
  3½" × WOF.

Light blue
- Cut 2 strips
  3½" × WOF.

- Cut 4 strips 1" × WOF.

Black
- Cut 1 strip 5" × WOF;
  subcut into 7 diamonds
  5" × 5".

- Cut 10 strips 1" × WOF.

Border print
- Cut 5 strips
  3½" × WOF.

Binding
- Cut 5 strips
  2¼" × WOF.

Construction

Refer to Getting Started (page 8) as needed.
Seam allowances are ¼" unless otherwise noted.

MAKE THE BLOCKS

The construction process of the triangle block in this quilt is different from the other blocks in this book. Because you use an odd shape, it is easier to make strip sets that include the black 1" strip, then cut out the shape. This saves a few steps for you and is much easier and quicker.

1. Copy the *Twilight* patterns A and B (page 61) and make a template for each pattern, using template plastic. Be sure to mark the templates with the black strip on the pattern.

2. Make light colored strip sets by sewing a black 1" × WOF strip between 2 light 3½" × WOF strips. Make 2 light purple sets, 2 light turquoise strip sets, and 1 light blue strip set. Press the seams toward the black strips.

3. With the fabric right side up, cut *Twilight* A shapes across each light strip set by rotating the template each time and matching the black fabric strip with the markings on the template. Cut 10 light purple A shapes, 10 light turquoise A shapes, and 6 light blue A shapes.

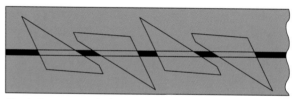

Cut A shapes across light strip sets.

4. Repeat Step 2 to make dark strip sets, using dark 3½" × WOF strips and black 1" × WOF strips. Press the seams away from the black. Make 2 dark purple strip sets, 2 dark turquoise strip sets, and 1 dark blue strip set.

5. With the fabric right side up, cut *Twilight* B shapes across each dark strip set by rotating the template each time and matching the black fabric strip with the markings on the template. Cut 10 dark purple A shapes, 10 dark turquoise A shapes, and 6 dark blue B shapes.

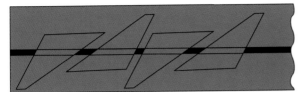

Cut B shapes across dark strip sets.

6. To make the whole diamonds, sew a light A shape to a dark B shape as shown. Make 10 purple diamonds, 10 turquoise diamonds, and 6 blue diamonds. Press the seams open.

Make a total of 26 diamonds— 10 purple, 10 turquoise, and 6 blue.

7. Referring to Slicing with a Ruler (page 9), slice the 7 black 5″ × 5″ diamonds in half lengthwise to create 14 long half-diamonds.

ASSEMBLE THE QUILT TOP

1. Referring to the quilt layout diagram (page 54), arrange the purple, turquoise, and blue diamonds with the black half-diamonds as shown.

2. Referring to Piecing a Hexagon (page 11), make the hexagons and partial hexagons. Press seams clock wise.

3. Sew the hexagons into a row and the partial hexagons into a second row. Press the seams open.

4. Referring to Joining Hexagon Rows and Columns (page 12), sew the rows together.

5. For the first border, sew the light blue 1″ × WOF strips together end to end. Cut 4 strips 1″ × 12″ for the 4 short sides and 2 strips 1″ × 48″ for the 2 long sides.

6. Sew a light blue 1″ × 12″ strip to 1 short side of the quilt center as shown. Trim the ends even with the quilt center. Continue adding the appropriate 1″ border strips to the quilt center in a clockwise direction as shown.

Sew first strip and trim.

Sew second strip and trim.

7. For the outside border, sew the print 3½″ × WOF strips together end to end. Cut 4 strips 3½″ × 16″ for the short sides and cut 2 strips 3½″ × 48″ for the long sides. Repeat Step 6 to add the outside border strips to the quilt.

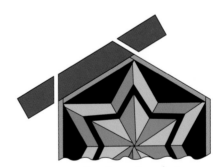

Sew first strip and trim.

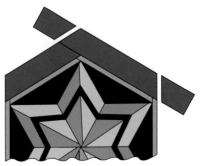

Sew second strip and trim.

FINISH

Refer to Quiltmaking Basics: How to Finish Your Quilt (page 55) as needed.

Layer, quilt, and bind as desired.

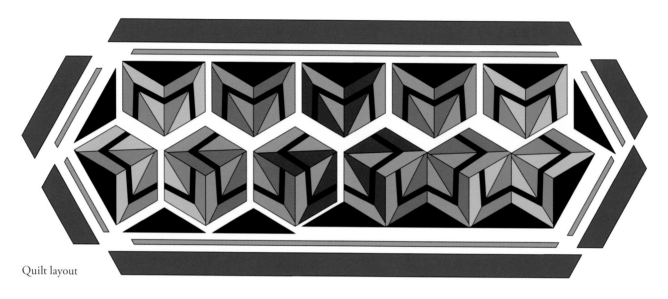

Quilt layout

COLOR OPTION AND VARIATION

Color option in Christmas colors

Twinkling Tricks by Rebecca C. Rittenhouse, 29″ × 33″, 2016

My daughter Rebecca made this table topper. Her variation has the stars overlapping in a circle rather than in a row.

QUILTMAKING BASICS:
How to Finish Your Quilt

General Guidelines

SEAM ALLOWANCES

A ¼″ seam allowance is used for most projects. It's a good idea to do a test seam before you begin sewing to check that your ¼″ is accurate. Accuracy is the key to successful piecing.

There is generally no need to backstitch. Ordinarily, seamlines will be crossed by another seam, which will anchor them. Sometimes you do need some tacking stitches when sewing Y-seams, for instance.

PRESSING

In general, press seams toward the darker fabric. Press lightly in an up-and-down motion. Avoid using a very hot iron or over-ironing, which can distort shapes and blocks. Be especially careful when pressing bias edges as they stretch easily.

Borders

When border strips are cut on the crosswise grain, piece the strips together to achieve the needed lengths.

In most cases the side borders are sewn on first. When you have finished the quilt top, measure it through the center vertically. This will be the length to cut the side borders. Place pins at the centers of all four sides of the quilt top, as well as in the center of each side border strip. Pin the side borders to the quilt top first, matching the center pins. Using a ¼″ seam allowance, sew the borders to the quilt top and press toward border.

Measure horizontally across the center of the quilt top including the side borders. This will be the length to cut the top and bottom borders. Repeat, pinning, sewing, and pressing.

Backing

Plan on making the backing a minimum of 8″ longer and wider than the quilt top. Piece, if necessary. Trim the selvages before you piece to the desired size.

To economize, piece the back from any leftover quilting fabrics or blocks in your collection.

Batting

The type of batting to use is a personal decision; consult your local quilt shop. Cut batting approximately 8″ longer and wider than your quilt top. Note that your batting choice will affect how much quilting is necessary for the quilt. Check the manufacturer's instructions to see how far apart the quilting lines can be.

Layering

Spread the backing wrong side up and tape the edges down with masking tape. (If you are working on carpet you can use T-pins to secure the backing to the carpet.) Center the batting on top, smoothing out any folds. Place the quilt top right side up on top of the batting and backing, making sure it is centered.

Basting

Basting keeps the quilt "sandwich" layers from shifting while you are quilting.

If you plan to machine quilt, pin baste the quilt layers together with safety pins placed about 3"–4" apart. Begin basting in the center and move toward the edges first in vertical, then horizontal, rows. Try not to pin directly on the intended quilting lines.

If you plan to hand quilt, baste the layers together with thread using a long needle and light-colored thread. Knot one end of the thread. Using stitches approximately the length of the needle, begin in the center and move out toward the edges in vertical and horizontal rows approximately 4" apart. Add 2 diagonal rows of basting.

Quilting

Quilting, whether by hand or machine, enhances the pieced or appliquéd design of the quilt. You may choose to quilt-in-the-ditch, echo the pieced or appliqué motifs, use patterns from quilting design books and stencils, or do your own free-motion quilting. Remember to check your batting manufacturer's recommendations for how close the quilting lines must be.

Binding

Trim excess batting and backing from the quilt even with the edges of the quilt top.

DOUBLE-FOLD STRAIGHT-GRAIN BINDING

If you want a ¼" finished binding, cut the binding strips 2¼" wide and piece them together with diagonal seams to make a continuous binding strip. Trim the seam allowance to ¼". Press the seams open.

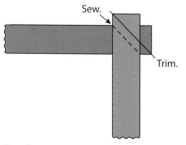

Sew from corner to corner.

Completed diagonal seam

Press the entire strip in half lengthwise with wrong sides together. With raw edges even, pin the binding to the front edge of the quilt a few inches away from a corner, and leave the first few inches of the binding unattached. Start sewing, using a ¼" seam allowance.

Stop ¼" away from the first corner (see next page, Fig. A), and backstitch one stitch. Lift the presser foot and needle. Rotate the quilt one-quarter turn. Fold the binding at a right angle so it extends straight above the quilt and the fold forms a 45° angle in the corner (see next page, Fig. B). Then bring the binding strip down even with the edge of the quilt (see next page, Fig. C). Begin sewing at the folded edge. Repeat in the same manner at all corners.

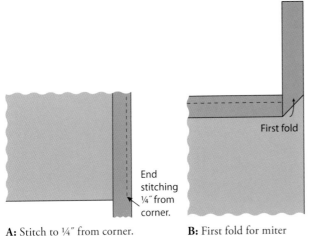

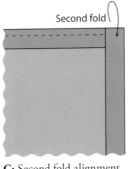

A: Stitch to ¼″ from corner.　　**B:** First fold for miter　　**C:** Second fold alignment

Continue stitching until you are back near the beginning of the binding strip. See Finishing the Binding Ends (next) for tips on finishing and hiding the raw edges of the ends of the binding.

FINISHING THE BINDING ENDS

Method 1

After stitching around the quilt, fold under the beginning tail of the binding strip ¼″ so that the raw edge will be inside the binding after it is turned to the back of the quilt. Place the end tail of the binding strip over the beginning folded end. Continue to attach the binding and stitch slightly beyond the starting stitches. Trim the excess binding. Fold the binding over the raw edges to the quilt back and hand stitch, mitering the corners.

Method 2

Refer to ctpub.com > scroll down to Support: Quiltmaking Basics and Sewing Tips > Completing a Binding with an Invisible Seam.

Fold the ending tail of the binding back on itself where it meets the beginning binding tail. From the fold, measure and mark the cut width of your binding strip. Cut the ending binding tail to this measurement. For example, if your binding is cut 2¼″ wide, measure from the fold on the ending tail of the binding 2¼″ and cut the binding tail to this length.

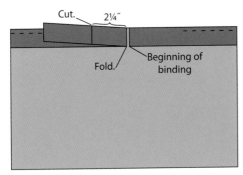

Cut binding tail.

Open both tails. Place one tail on top of the other tail at right angles, right sides together. Mark a diagonal line from corner to corner and stitch on the line. Check that you've done it correctly and that the binding fits the quilt; then trim the seam allowance to ¼″. Press open.

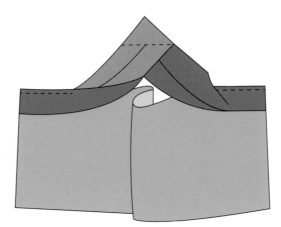

Stitch ends of binding diagonally.

Refold the binding and stitch this binding section in place on the quilt. Fold the binding over the raw edges to the quilt back and hand stitch.

PATTERNS

Just a Square (page 13)

Compass (page 33)

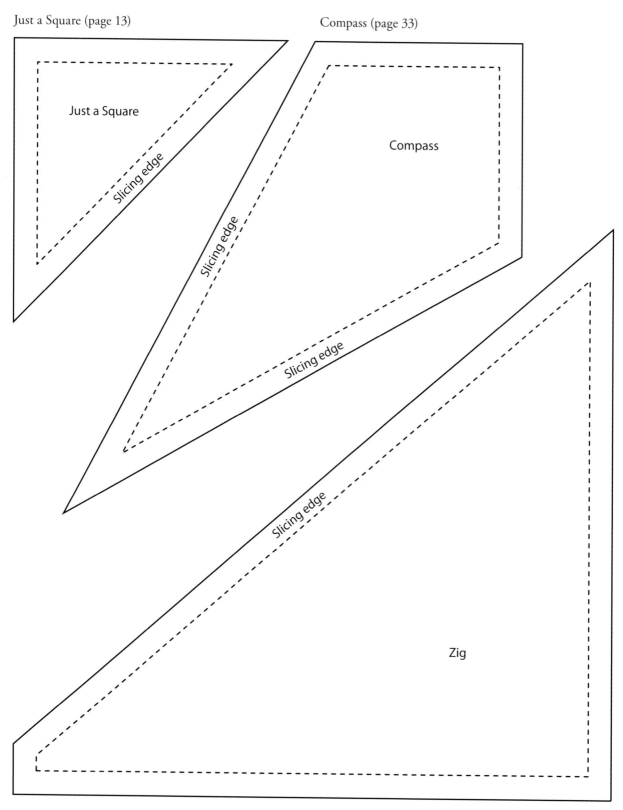

Just a Square

Slicing edge

Slicing edge

Compass

Slicing edge

Slicing edge

Zig

Zig and Zag (page 17)

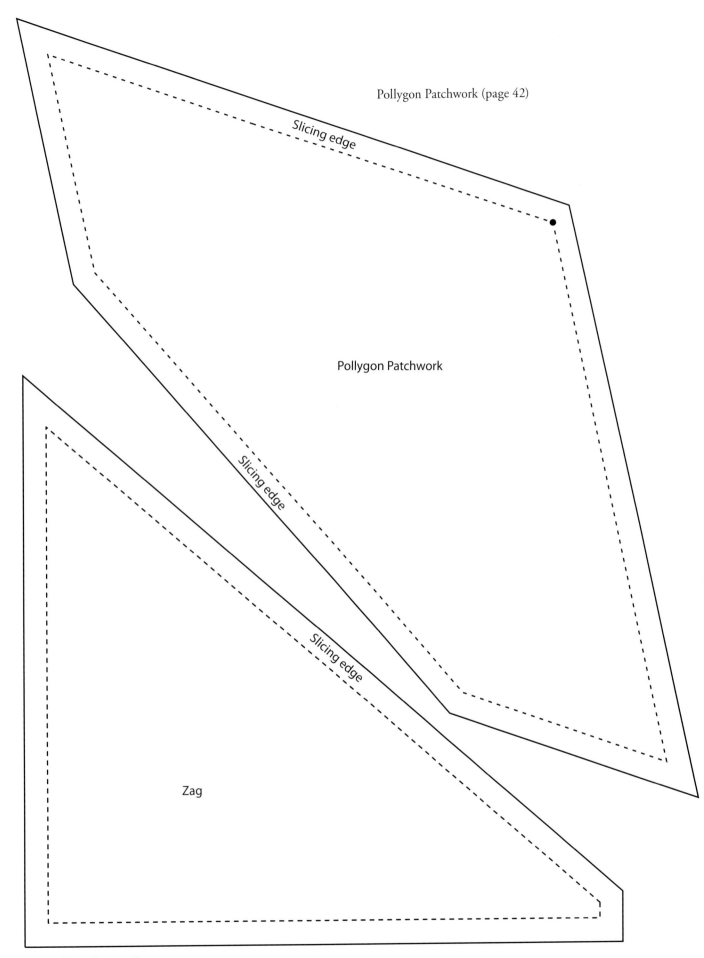

Pollygon Patchwork (page 42)

Slicing edge

Pollygon Patchwork

Slicing edge

Slicing edge

Zag

Zig and Zag (page 17)

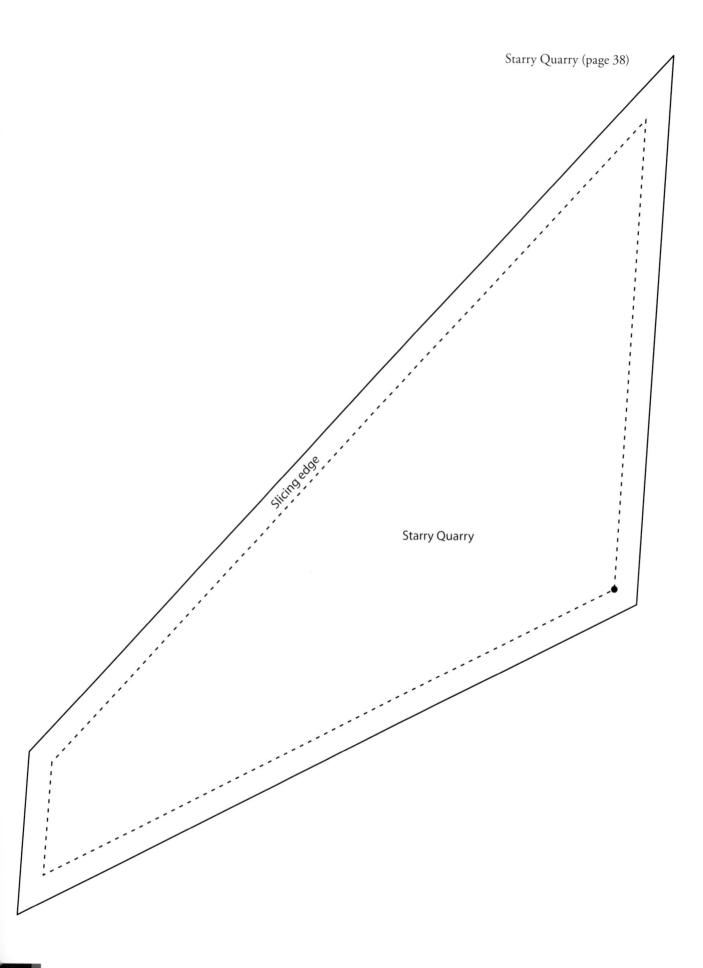

Slicing edge

Starry Quarry

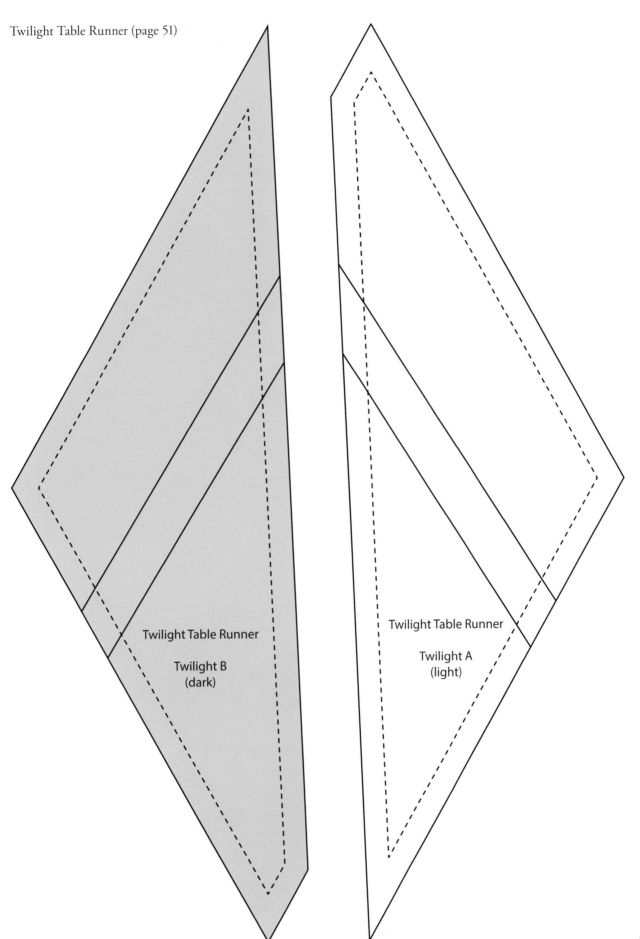

Twilight Table Runner

Twilight B
(dark)

Twilight Table Runner

Twilight A
(light)

ABOUT THE AUTHOR

Barbara H. Cline started creating quilts in her teens. Since then, she has had more than 31 years of experience teaching quiltmaking classes at a local sewing shop and creating beautiful quilts and patterns. Barbara worked at The Clothes Line fabric shop (now called Patchwork Plus) in Virginia from fifth grade until she married and had children. She became a stay-at-home mother who pieced quilt tops to sell when she had time. When her youngest child entered kindergarten, she started working part-time at The Clothes Line again.

Barbara currently teaches classes at Patchwork Plus and Sew Classic Fabrics and loves to design and piece wallhangings and quilts from her home in Shenandoah Valley, Virginia. Her quilts have been shown and have won ribbons in various quilt shows and contests.

Barbara comes from a close-knit Mennonite family of quilters; her grandmother Vera Heatwole taught her daughters, granddaughters, great-granddaughters, great-great-granddaughters, and daughters-in-law to quilt.

Every year the women gather for a sewing retreat, where they quilt, sew, and follow other creative pursuits. The family members and their quilts were featured in the Virginia Quilt Museum's exhibition Five Generations of Mennonite Quilts.

To learn more about Barbara, visit her website: delightfulpiecing.com

Also by Barbara H. Cline:

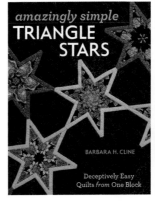 

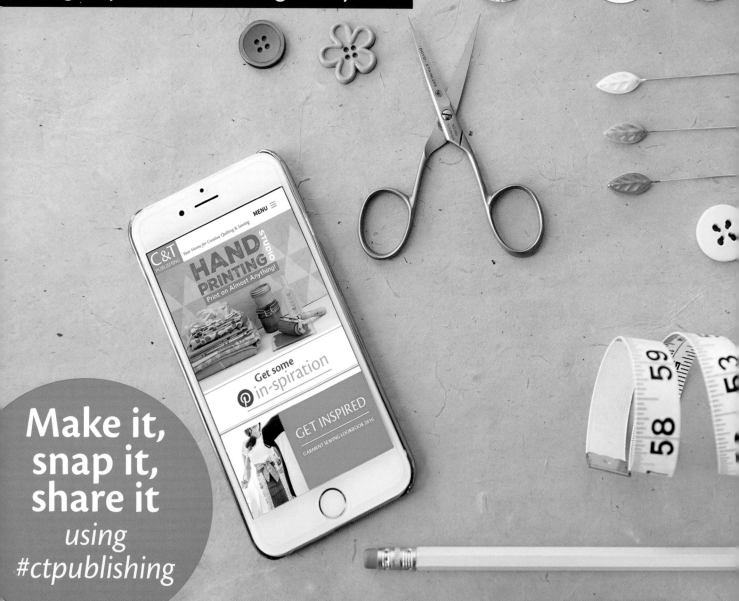